JUSTIN JEFFERSON: The Boy Who Danced His Way to Football Fame(A Biography Book for Kids)

Linda R. Crouse

• AUTHOR BIOGRAPHY

Linda R. Crouse is an experienced children's author with a passion for sharing inspiring stories about real-life heroes who capture the hearts and imaginations of young readers. With a special focus on sports biographies, Linda creates engaging books that encourage kids to dream big, work hard, and have fun while learning valuable life lessons.

Linda's love for storytelling began when she was a child, fascinated by the achievements of athletes who defied the odds. As an adult, she turned that fascination into a career, writing books that highlight the journeys of extraordinary athletes, making their stories accessible and exciting for kids. Her goal is to help children understand that behind every great player is a story of perseverance, teamwork, and believing in yourself.

In Justin Jefferson: The Boy Who Danced His Way to Football Fame, Linda brings to life the story of NFL star Justin Jefferson, blending fun facts and important lessons into a story that motivates young readers to follow their passions. With simple language and exciting details, Linda shows kids how Justin's dedication to football and his signature Griddy dance made him a fan favorite, on and off the field.

When she's not writing, Linda enjoys watching sports, spending time outdoors, and encouraging young readers to explore their potential. She believes that stories have the power to inspire, and her books aim to spark that inspiration in children everywhere.

Linda R. Crouse continues to write biographies of notable athletes, helping young readers connect with their favorite sports stars while learning the value of hard work, kindness, and never giving up on their dreams.

• TABLE OF CONTENTS

● INTRODUCTION

Have you ever dreamed of being a football star, catching touchdowns in front of thousands of cheering fans? Or maybe you've watched a game and wondered how players like Justin Jefferson became so great at what they do. Well, you're about to discover the exciting journey of one of football's brightest young stars, Justin Jefferson!

Justin isn't just known for his amazing skills on the football field, he's also famous for his unique way of celebrating, the Griddy dance! In this book, we'll dive into Justin's life story, starting from when he was just a kid like you, with big dreams and a love for football. He worked hard, practiced every day, and chased his dreams to become one of the best wide receivers in the NFL.

But Justin's journey wasn't always easy. He faced challenges along the way, including doubts from others and tough competition. However, he never gave up. Through determination, hard work, and a love for the game, Justin showed the world that with passion and dedication, you can achieve anything.

This book is written especially for kids like you, who might be dreaming of becoming a sports star or reaching your own goals. You'll learn about how Justin grew up, what inspired him, and how he pushed through the tough times to become the football hero he is today. You'll also read about some of his most amazing moments on the field, from his time playing with his brothers in the backyard to making incredible catches in the NFL.

Not only will you discover the story of his rise to fame, but you'll also find out what makes Justin special off the field. Justin is more than just a football player—he's also a role model who believes in helping others, working as a team, and staying positive no matter what. His story will show you how important it is to be kind, believe in yourself, and never give up on your dreams.

One of the most exciting parts of Justin's story is how he introduced the Griddy dance to the world. You'll read about how this fun and energetic dance became famous after one of his big touchdown catches. Now, kids everywhere are doing the Griddy, celebrating just like Justin when he scores. It's a reminder that being yourself and having fun can make you stand out, just like it did for him.

Throughout the book, you'll follow Justin's journey from a small town in Louisiana to the biggest football stages in the country. You'll read about his high school days, where he started to show his talent and potential, and how he went on to play for Louisiana State University (LSU). There, Justin worked hard and became a champion, helping his team win a national title.

Then came the moment that changed everything—Justin's name was called in the

NFL Draft, and he became a member of the Minnesota Vikings! His dreams of playing professional football had come true, but his story was only beginning. In the NFL, Justin quickly became one of the league's top players, setting records and winning the hearts of fans everywhere with his skills and fun personality.

As you read Justin's story, you'll see how he worked through challenges and always kept pushing forward, even when things got tough. You'll also learn that success isn't just about winning games or scoring touchdowns. It's about staying true to who you are, working well with others, and remembering to have fun along the way.

Justin Jefferson's story isn't just for kids who love football, it's for anyone with big dreams. His life shows us that no matter where you start, if you work hard, stay focused, and believe in yourself, you can achieve amazing things. And along the way, it's important to remember to dance, smile, and enjoy the journey, just like Justin does with every touchdown.

Whether you're a football fan or someone who loves inspiring stories, this book will take you through Justin Jefferson's incredible rise to fame. From his early days as a boy with big dreams to becoming one of the most exciting players in the NFL, Justin's story is full of fun, hard work, and unforgettable moments.

So, get ready to dive into the world of football, fun, and big dreams. By the end of this book, you'll know why Justin Jefferson is not just a football star, but a hero for kids everywhere. His journey shows us that with the right mindset, anything is possible.

Let's jump into the story of Justin Jefferson: The Boy Who Danced His Way to Football Fame and see how one boy's dreams turned into a reality that's bigger and better than he ever imagined.

• CHAPTER 1: MEET JUSTIN JEFFERSON : AND WHY IS HE SO AWESOME?

Justin Jefferson is one of the brightest young stars in the world of football today. As a wide receiver for the Minnesota Vikings in the National Football League (NFL), he has quickly risen to fame thanks to his incredible skills, athleticism, and personality. But what makes Justin so awesome? It's not just his ability to catch footballs or score touchdowns; it's his journey, his attitude, and the impact he's making both on and off the field.

A Humble Beginning

Justin was born on June 16, 1999, in St. Rose, Louisiana, a small town just outside New Orleans. He grew up in a family where football was a big deal. His two older brothers, Jordan and Rickey, were also passionate about the sport and played at high levels. With football being such an important part of family life, Justin naturally developed a love for the game from a young age. He spent countless hours playing in the backyard with his brothers, learning how to catch, throw, and run.

Although he was always determined and hardworking, Justin didn't have an easy path to becoming a professional football player. During his early years in high school, he wasn't the most talked-about player. In fact, he was considered too small and too light to be a serious contender. But instead of giving up, Justin used these doubts as motivation. He trained harder, stayed focused, and made sure he was ready when his chance came.

High School to College

By the time Justin reached his senior year at Destrehan High School, he was starting to make waves. His talent for catching footballs and his speed on the field caught the attention of college scouts. Despite not being heavily recruited early on, Justin earned a spot at Louisiana State

University (LSU), where his journey to greatness truly began.

At LSU, Justin proved that hard work pays off. He played a significant role in the team's success, but it was in 2019 that everything came together. That year, LSU had an incredible season, winning the national championship. Justin was one of the team's standout players, catching 111 passes for 1,540 yards and 18 touchdowns. His performance in the national spotlight solidified his place as one of the top wide receivers in the country.

The NFL Draft and Joining the Vikings

After his impressive college career, Justin entered the 2020 NFL Draft. On draft day, he was selected by the Minnesota Vikings as the 22nd overall pick. For Justin, this was a dream come true. Not only was he heading to the NFL, but he was joining a team with a rich history and passionate fans.

Once Justin stepped onto the field as a rookie, it didn't take long for everyone to realize just how special he was. In his first season, he set records, scored touchdowns, and quickly became one of the most exciting players to watch. His ability to run fast, make difficult catches look easy, and celebrate with his now-famous "Griddy" dance made him a fan favorite.

What Makes Justin Jefferson Special?

So, what exactly makes Justin Jefferson so awesome? Here are a few key things:

1. Incredible Work Ethic: Justin's success didn't come overnight. It's a result of years of hard work and dedication. He never let setbacks stop him and always found a way to improve his game.

2. Amazing Skills: Justin has an uncanny ability to make spectacular catches, outrun defenders, and create opportunities for his team to score.

His football IQ is high, and he's always thinking one step ahead of the opposition.

3. A Positive Attitude: Throughout his journey, Justin has remained humble and positive. He's grateful for the opportunities he's had and always takes time to thank his coaches, teammates, and family for their support.

4. The "Griddy" Dance: One of the things that makes Justin stand out is his famous touchdown celebration, the "Griddy." This dance, which originated in Louisiana, has become Justin's signature move and has been adopted by fans and players all over the NFL. It's a fun way for Justin to celebrate his success and show off his personality.

5. Inspiring Others: Justin's story is one of determination and perseverance. He shows kids and young athletes that it's okay to be underestimated as long as you keep working hard. His journey from a small town to NFL

stardom proves that with the right mindset, anything is possible.

Justin's greatness doesn't stop when he leaves the football field. He's known for being a kind and generous person who enjoys giving back to his community. He's used his platform to support various causes and has made it a point to inspire the next generation of athletes. Whether he's signing autographs for young fans, speaking to kids about the importance of education and hard work, or participating in charity events, Justin is always looking for ways to make a positive impact.

Justin Jefferson's story is just beginning. At such a young age, he's already accomplished more than most football players dream of, but he's far from finished. He continues to push himself to new heights, always striving to be better. His dedication to his craft and his passion for the game ensure that his future in the NFL is bright.

As Justin continues to grow and evolve as a player, fans and kids everywhere are watching closely. His journey is an inspiration, showing that with hard work, heart, and a little bit of flair, you can achieve your dreams. So, why is Justin Jefferson so awesome? It's because he's more than just a football star, he's a role model, a trailblazer, and someone who never gave up on his dreams.

• CHAPTER 2: GROWING UP WITH BIG DREAMS

Justin Jefferson's journey to becoming an NFL superstar didn't begin with fame, big stadiums, or highlight reels. It started in the small town of St. Rose, Louisiana, where he grew up surrounded by family and football. Born on June 16, 1999, Justin was the youngest of three boys in a family that lived and breathed the game. His childhood was filled with football dreams and backyard games, which would ultimately shape his future.

A Family of Football

In the Jefferson household, football was more than just a weekend sport; it was a way of life. Justin's two older brothers, Jordan and Rickey, were passionate about football, and their love for the game had a strong influence on him. Jordan was a standout quarterback for Louisiana State University (LSU), and Rickey also played at the college level. With both brothers blazing their own trails in football, it was no surprise that young Justin dreamed of following in their footsteps.

From an early age, Justin was determined to become a great football player. He spent countless hours practicing in the yard with his brothers, learning how to catch, throw, and run with the football. Their games were intense and competitive, and they pushed Justin to develop the skills he would later use to succeed on much bigger stages. Those backyard battles were crucial in helping him build the confidence and resilience needed to chase his dreams.

Early Challenges

While growing up with older brothers who were football stars may sound like an advantage, Justin faced challenges of his own. Unlike his brothers, who had the size and strength typical of football players, Justin was smaller and lighter during his early years. This sometimes made it hard for him to stand out on the field. Many people doubted whether he had what it took to follow in his brothers' footsteps, but Justin didn't let that stop him.

Instead of being discouraged, Justin used these doubts as motivation. He didn't complain or give up; he worked harder. Even when he wasn't the biggest player, he made sure to be the most determined. He spent hours after school working on his speed, agility, and catching skills. He practiced running routes over and over again, perfecting every move so that when the time came, he would be ready to prove his doubters wrong.

What set Justin apart, even from a young age, was his unwavering belief in himself and his dreams. He didn't just dream of being a good football player—he dreamed of being one of the best. Even as a kid, Justin envisioned himself catching passes in the NFL, celebrating touchdowns, and making big plays in front of thousands of cheering fans. These dreams were vivid, and they fueled his work ethic.

One of the things that helped Justin stay focused on his dreams was his family's support. His parents, John and Elaine Jefferson, always encouraged him to keep working hard and to never lose sight of what he wanted to achieve. They believed in his potential and made sure he had every opportunity to succeed, whether that meant driving him to practices, attending his games, or giving him pep talks when things got tough.

As Justin entered high school at Destrehan High School in Louisiana, he began to take his football dreams more seriously. But even then, the road wasn't easy. During his freshman and sophomore years, Justin was still considered too small by many coaches and scouts. Despite having great hands and good speed, he wasn't seen as a top prospect. But that didn't matter to Justin. He was determined to prove everyone wrong.

By his junior year, Justin had grown both physically and mentally. He started to develop into a standout wide receiver, catching passes that seemed impossible to others. His confidence on the field grew with every game, and his determination to succeed became even stronger. He knew he had what it took to play at the next level, and he was going to make sure that everyone else saw it too.

During his senior year, Justin's hard work began to pay off. He became a key player for Destrehan, helping his team win games and impressing college scouts along the way. His ability to make difficult catches and outrun defenders made him a star in the eyes of his coaches and teammates. Finally, after years of hard work and perseverance, Justin earned a scholarship to play football at Louisiana State University (LSU), the same school where his brother Jordan had played.

Getting into LSU was a major turning point in Justin's life. It wasn't just about continuing his football career—it was about proving to himself and others that dreams do come true with enough effort and belief. At LSU, Justin had the chance to showcase his talents on a much larger stage. But even then, his journey wasn't without obstacles.

During his first year at LSU, Justin wasn't a starter. In fact, he spent most of the season on the sidelines, watching other players get the spotlight. But instead of getting discouraged, Justin used this time to learn. He studied the game, watched the veterans, and worked on his skills. By the time his second season rolled around, he was ready to make his mark.

And make his mark he did. In his second year at LSU, Justin exploded onto the scene, becoming one of the team's most reliable receivers. His hard work, dedication, and relentless pursuit of his dream were finally paying off. He was catching passes, scoring touchdowns, and helping LSU win big games. By the time his college career was over, Justin had helped lead LSU to a national championship, cementing his place as one of the top wide receivers in the country.

Justin Jefferson's journey from a small-town kid with big dreams to an NFL superstar is more than just a story about football. It's a lesson in perseverance, hard work, and the power of believing in yourself. Justin didn't have the perfect start, but he never let that hold him back. He faced challenges, doubts, and setbacks along the way, but he always kept his eye on his goal.

One of the biggest lessons from Justin's story is that dreams are worth chasing, no matter how big they are. He never let his size, the opinions of others, or any obstacles stand in the way of what he wanted to achieve. He believed in his dream of playing in the NFL, and he was willing to put in the effort to make that dream a reality.

For kids reading Justin's story, the message is clear: No matter where you come from, how big or small you are, or how many challenges you face, you can achieve your dreams if you work hard, stay focused, and never give up. Justin Jefferson's journey shows that with determination and a belief in yourself, anything is possible. His story is a reminder that big dreams can come true, no matter how impossible they may seem at first.

• CHAPTER 3: FOOTBALL FUN IN THE BACKYARD: HOW JUSTIN STARTED PLAYING FOOTBALL WITH HIS BROTHERS

Growing up in St. Rose, Louisiana, Justin Jefferson's early life revolved around two significant things: family and football. As the youngest of three brothers, he found himself surrounded by role models and competition from an early age. His two older brothers, Jordan and Rickey, were passionate about the sport, and their love for football became a central theme in Justin's upbringing. This familial bond would lay the foundation for Justin's journey to becoming an NFL star, showcasing the power of sibling rivalry, teamwork, and fun in shaping his athletic career.

The Backyard Playground

For Justin, the backyard served as a personal football field where he first learned to love the game. With a modest yard and a goalpost made from whatever they could find, Justin and his brothers transformed their home into a playground for football. They would spend hours outside, throwing the ball back and forth, practicing catches, and running routes. It was in this environment that Justin honed his skills and developed a deep appreciation for the game.

The backyard was more than just a place to play; it was where Justin learned valuable lessons about teamwork, strategy, and perseverance. Jordan and Rickey would often set up mini-games, creating competitions that ignited Justin's competitive spirit. These games were intense, filled with laughter and occasional arguments, but they also strengthened their bond as brothers. Justin was always eager to prove himself, and this drive pushed him to become a better player.

Learning from the Best

Justin admired his brothers immensely. Jordan, being a talented quarterback, often demonstrated how to throw precise passes and make strategic decisions on the field. Rickey, on the other hand, was known for his speed and agility. He showed Justin how to run routes effectively and evade defenders. As the youngest, Justin absorbed everything like a sponge, taking notes from their techniques and trying to implement them into his game.

During these backyard sessions, Justin quickly learned that football was about more than just individual skills. It was about understanding the game and working as a unit. His brothers encouraged him to communicate effectively, signaling plays and calling out strategies. They taught him the importance of trust on the field, emphasizing that even the best players need to rely on their teammates to succeed.

Sibling Rivalry

Sibling rivalry played a significant role in Justin's early football experiences. Every time they stepped into the backyard, the competition was fierce. They kept score of every catch and every touchdown, turning each practice into a mini championship. Justin was determined to keep up with his brothers, and he often pushed himself to improve.

The friendly rivalry taught Justin valuable lessons about resilience. There were moments of frustration when he struggled to make a catch or missed a play, but he learned to bounce back and keep trying. His brothers were his biggest motivators, always reminding him that every mistake was an opportunity to learn. This mindset became integral to Justin's development, shaping his character both on and off the field.

The Power of Imagination

In addition to structured games, the backyard was also a place for creativity. Justin and his brothers often invented new games, combining elements of football with their own imaginative twists. They would create obstacles, set up challenges, and even incorporate other sports like basketball and soccer into their playtime. This allowed Justin to develop a diverse skill set and keep the game fun and exciting.

Their imagination often turned ordinary days into grand adventures. Whether it was pretending to be NFL stars or creating elaborate storylines for their games, Justin's creativity kept him engaged and motivated. This imaginative play not only made him a well-rounded athlete but also reinforced the idea that sports are meant to be enjoyable.

Gaining Confidence

As Justin continued to play in the backyard, he began to build confidence in his abilities. Each successful catch and touchdown celebrated by his brothers added to his self-esteem. The support he received from Jordan and Rickey instilled a belief in him that he could succeed.

He learned that confidence is crucial in sports, as it allows athletes to perform at their best.

Their encouragement also pushed Justin to take risks. He learned to trust his instincts and try new moves on the field. This confidence translated into his schoolyard games and eventually into organized football. The lessons he learned from playing with his brothers gave him a solid foundation that he would carry throughout his athletic career.

Transition to Organized Football

Eventually, Justin's backyard games paved the way for his transition to organized football. As he entered middle school, he began to play for his local youth football team. His skills had improved significantly, thanks to the countless hours spent in the backyard with his brothers. Justin quickly became a standout player, impressing coaches and teammates with his speed, agility, and catching ability.

His early experiences gave him a unique edge. While many of his peers were just starting to learn the basics of the game, Justin had been playing for years. He was comfortable on the field and understood the nuances of teamwork and strategy. This head start allowed him to excel, further igniting his passion for football.

The Impact of Family Support

The support of his family was crucial throughout Justin's journey. His parents, John and Elaine Jefferson, encouraged their sons' love for football. They attended every game, cheered from the sidelines, and celebrated their accomplishments. This unwavering support created an environment where Justin felt safe to pursue his dreams.

Family gatherings often turned into discussions about football, with stories being shared about past games and players. These conversations kept Justin motivated and helped him visualize his goals. He learned that with dedication and a supportive network, dreams could turn into reality.

Playing football with his brothers instilled a strong work ethic in Justin. He understood that talent alone wasn't enough to succeed; it required hard work and discipline. After school, he would often head straight to the backyard to practice, even if his brothers weren't around. He set personal goals, challenging himself to improve his speed and catching ability.

This work ethic became apparent as he progressed through high school. Justin was known for being one of the first to arrive at practice and the last to leave. He approached training with the same intensity he had in the backyard, always seeking ways to refine his skills and grow as a player.

The journey wasn't always smooth. As Justin entered high school, he faced new challenges, including tougher competition and injuries. However, the resilience he developed while playing with his brothers prepared him for these obstacles. He learned to embrace challenges as opportunities for growth rather than setbacks.

Whenever faced with adversity, Justin would think back to those backyard games. He remembered the times he struggled but ultimately triumphed. This mindset kept him grounded and focused on his goals, allowing him to push through tough times.

Justin Jefferson's journey from playing in the backyard to becoming a professional football player is a testament to the power of family, hard work, and perseverance. The lessons he learned while playing with his brothers laid the groundwork for his future success.

Today, Justin continues to inspire young athletes around the world. His story serves as a reminder that the roots of greatness often lie in simple moments of fun and family bonding. For every child who dreams of becoming a star athlete, Justin's experiences highlight the importance of support, practice, and the joy of playing the game.

As Justin continues to shine on the field, he remains grateful for those early days in the backyard—days filled with laughter, competition, and the unwavering support of his brothers. His journey is a powerful reminder that big dreams often begin in the most unexpected places, and with determination, anything is possible.

• CHAPTER 4: HIGH SCHOOL HERO: JUSTIN'S FIRST TASTE OF BEING A FOOTBALL STAR

As Justin Jefferson entered high school, he was filled with excitement and anticipation. He had spent countless hours playing football in his backyard with his brothers, but now it was time to take his passion to the next level. Attending Destrehan High School in Louisiana, Justin was eager to join the school's football team and make a name for himself on the field.

Joining the Team

Walking onto the field for the first time as a freshman was a thrilling experience for Justin. He was greeted by the sights and sounds of a bustling football practice, coaches shouting instructions, players running drills, and the smell of freshly cut grass. Justin knew that this was where he belonged. He quickly signed up for the junior varsity team, ready to prove his skills and dedication.

The team was filled with talented players, some of whom were older and had already established themselves as stars. Justin was determined to show everyone what he could do. Despite being younger and smaller than some of his teammates, he had confidence in his abilities and was ready to work hard to earn his place on the team.

Hard Work and Determination

Justin's commitment to improving his game was evident from day one. He arrived at practice early, ready to work on his skills before the official practice started. He practiced catching passes, running routes, and improving his speed. The coaches took notice of his enthusiasm and talent. They appreciated his strong work ethic and encouraged him to keep pushing himself.

One of the first things Justin learned was the importance of teamwork. He quickly formed friendships with his teammates, bonding over shared goals and aspirations. They worked together to improve, pushing each other to become better players. Justin realized that football was not just about individual talent; it was about supporting one another and working as a cohesive unit.

Learning from Coaches

Under the guidance of his coaches, Justin began to understand the strategies and techniques that could take his game to the next level. His coaches provided valuable feedback, helping him refine his skills. They taught him how to read defenses, make quick decisions, and use his speed to his advantage. Justin listened intently, soaking up all the information he could.

He also learned the importance of mental preparation. Football is as much a mental game as it is a physical one. Justin spent time studying playbooks, memorizing routes, and understanding the game's intricacies. This dedication helped him feel more confident during games, knowing he had put in the effort to prepare.

Stepping onto the Field

As the season progressed, Justin earned a spot on the varsity team. The first time he stepped onto the field during a game was exhilarating. The stadium was filled with cheering fans, and the atmosphere buzzed with energy. Justin could feel his heart racing as he put on his jersey, a symbol of the hard work he had put in.

When the coach called his name, Justin ran onto the field with excitement. He was ready to show everyone what he could do. The adrenaline surged through him as the game began, and he quickly got into the flow of the action. His training and preparation paid off, and he played with confidence.

A Rising Star

Justin's performances on the field did not go unnoticed. He quickly became a standout player for his team, making impressive catches and scoring touchdowns. His speed and agility set him apart from others, and he started to gain recognition as a rising star. Fans and teammates cheered for him, and Justin felt a sense of pride in his accomplishments.

As he scored his first touchdown, the crowd erupted in cheers. The joy of crossing into the end zone was exhilarating. It was a moment he would never forget, a culmination of all his hard work, dedication, and dreams coming true. This touchdown solidified his place as a key player on the team and fueled his passion for the sport even more.

Despite his success, Justin faced challenges along the way. There were tough games where the team struggled to perform, and losses were difficult to swallow. However, Justin learned that these moments were also opportunities for growth. He understood that setbacks were a part of sports, and it was essential to remain resilient and focused on improving.

During practice, Justin would reflect on the mistakes made in games, seeking ways to do better next time. His teammates rallied around each other, encouraging one another to push through tough times. This support system was crucial in helping Justin maintain a positive attitude, even when faced with adversity.

Building Leadership Skills

As the season continued, Justin's leadership skills began to shine. He encouraged his teammates during practices, always pushing them to give their best effort. He realized that being a good player also meant being a good teammate. Justin helped younger players learn the ropes, sharing tips and tricks he had learned over the years.

His coaches recognized his leadership potential and started to give him more responsibility on the field. They asked him to help call plays and communicate with his teammates during games. This was a significant honor for Justin and showed that his hard work was paying off. He embraced this new role, understanding that being a leader meant leading by example and motivating others to reach their full potential.

Throughout this journey, Justin's family remained his biggest supporters. His parents attended every game, cheering him on from the stands. They celebrated his successes and helped him through the tough times. Justin knew that he could always count on their encouragement, which motivated him to give his best effort.

After games, they would discuss his performance, focusing on what went well and areas for improvement. This open communication helped Justin stay grounded and focused on his goals. He was grateful for the unwavering support of his family, which fueled his desire to succeed.

As the football season approached its end, Justin and his teammates were gearing up for the final game. The excitement was palpable, and everyone was determined to finish strong. Justin knew that this game would be a significant opportunity to showcase all he had learned and accomplished throughout the season.

When the day of the final game arrived, the atmosphere was electric. The stadium was packed with fans, all eager to see the team play. Justin felt a mix of nerves and excitement, but he was ready to take on the challenge. He had trained hard and knew that he could rely on his skills and instincts.

By the end of the season, Justin had established himself as a high school football hero. His hard work and dedication had paid off, leading to impressive statistics and accolades. More importantly, he had forged lasting friendships and created unforgettable memories with his teammates.

As the final whistle blew, Justin reflected on the journey he had taken. He realized that football was more than just a game; it had taught him valuable life lessons about teamwork, perseverance, and leadership. His experiences on the field inspired him to continue pursuing his dreams, both in sports and in life.

With high school behind him, Justin was ready to take the next step in his football career. He dreamed of playing at the collegiate level and eventually in the NFL. His time as a high school hero had set the stage for an exciting future, filled with challenges and opportunities.

As he prepared for the next chapter, Justin carried with him the lessons he had learned on the field and the love and support of his family. He was determined to continue working hard, staying focused, and chasing his dreams. Justin Jefferson had taken his first taste of being a football star, and there was no stopping him now. The journey ahead was bright, and he was excited to see where it would lead him next.

• CHAPTER 5: COLLEGE DAYS AT LSU: HOW JUSTIN BECAME A CHAMPION AT LOUISIANA STATE UNIVERSITY

After an incredible high school football career, Justin Jefferson was ready to take the next big step in his journey. He earned a scholarship to Louisiana State University (LSU), one of the top college football programs in the country. This was a dream come true for Justin, who had always wanted to play football at a big university. Little did he know, these college days would become some of the most exciting and challenging times of his life.

Arrival at LSU

When Justin arrived at LSU, he was filled with a mix of excitement and nerves. The campus was vast and buzzing with energy. He saw students everywhere, walking to classes, hanging out with friends, and cheering for the Tigers, LSU's mascot. The first thing he noticed was the incredible support for the football team. LSU was known for its passionate fans, and Justin could feel the excitement in the air.

On his first day, he met his fellow teammates and coaches. Everyone welcomed him with open arms, and he quickly felt like part of the team. The coaches were excited to have him on board, and Justin was eager to learn and grow as a player. He knew that he would need to work harder than ever to succeed at this level.

Training Hard

College football was different from high school. The competition was tougher, and the players were bigger and faster. Justin knew he had to put in extra effort to stand out. The practices were intense, filled with drills, scrimmages, and conditioning exercises. Justin pushed himself every day, determined to improve his skills and prove he belonged on the team.

One of the most valuable lessons Justin learned during his time at LSU was the importance of teamwork. He quickly realized that success on the field depended on how well he worked with his teammates. Justin developed strong friendships with his fellow wide receivers, who shared tips and tricks to help each other improve. They would often stay after practice to run additional routes and catch passes, working together to become better players.

Learning from Coaches

The coaching staff at LSU was top-notch, with years of experience and a deep understanding of the game. Justin soaked up their knowledge like a sponge. They taught him about reading defenses, running precise routes, and improving his catching technique. Justin appreciated their guidance and used their advice to refine his skills.

His coaches also emphasized the importance of mental preparation. Football is as much about strategy and planning as it is about physical ability. Justin learned to study game film, analyze opponents, and develop a game plan for each match. This mental preparation helped him feel more confident during games, allowing him to perform at his best.

First Game Day Excitement

As the season approached, the excitement grew. Justin could hardly contain his anticipation for his first college game. The energy in the locker room was electric, and he could feel the adrenaline pumping through his veins. He put on his jersey, proudly displaying the LSU colors, and joined his teammates as they prepared to take the field.

When they ran out of the tunnel onto the field, Justin was amazed. The stadium was packed with fans, all wearing purple and gold, cheering and waving flags. The atmosphere was unlike anything he had ever experienced. As the band played the fight song and the crowd roared,

Justin felt an overwhelming sense of pride and determination.

Making an Impact

Justin's hard work paid off, and he quickly became an essential part of the team. In his first game, he had several impressive catches and made a significant impact on the field. The coaches and fans took notice, and Justin felt a rush of excitement each time he caught a pass. He was living his dream and loving every moment of it.

As the season continued, Justin continued to shine. He developed a strong connection with the team's quarterback, who trusted him to make big plays. They practiced together to perfect their timing and communication, allowing them to execute impressive passes during games. The chemistry between them was incredible, and it showed in their performances on the field.

However, Justin also faced challenges during his college career. There were tough losses and difficult games that tested his resilience. Sometimes he struggled with self-doubt, wondering if he could compete at this level. But with the support of his teammates and coaches, Justin learned to bounce back from setbacks. They encouraged him to focus on the positives and reminded him of his talent and hard work.

Through determination and perseverance, Justin continued to improve. He spent extra time reviewing game footage and working on his technique. Each challenge became an opportunity for growth, and he became more motivated to succeed. Justin learned that every setback was a chance to rise stronger, and this mindset helped him become a better player.

As the seasons progressed, Justin's hard work and dedication began to pay off. He earned numerous accolades for his outstanding performances, including awards for being one of the top wide receivers in the country. Fans cheered for him, and his name became well-known in college football circles. Justin felt grateful for the recognition but remained focused on helping his team win.

His most memorable achievement came during his final season at LSU. The team made it to the College Football Playoff, and Justin played a crucial role in leading them to victory. The atmosphere during the playoff games was electric, with fans cheering louder than ever. Justin stepped up to the challenge, making incredible catches and helping the team secure its place in the championship game.

The championship game was the highlight of Justin's college career. As the day approached, excitement filled the air. The team practiced diligently, preparing for their toughest opponent yet. Justin was determined to give his best performance, knowing that this was an opportunity to leave a lasting legacy at LSU.

On game day, the stadium was packed with fans, and the energy was palpable. Justin felt a mix of nerves and excitement as he put on his uniform. He joined his teammates in the locker room, where they shared words of encouragement and reminded each other to stay focused.

When the game began, Justin quickly got into the flow of the action. He made several critical catches, helping the team score important points. The game was intense, but Justin remained calm and focused. With each play, he knew he was one step closer to achieving his dream of becoming a champion.

In the final moments of the game, with the score tied, Justin made a spectacular catch that set up the winning touchdown. The crowd erupted in cheers as the team celebrated their hard-earned victory. Justin felt a rush of emotions—joy, relief, and pride. They had done it! He was now a champion.

After the championship victory, Justin's future was bright. He had proven himself as one of the best players in college football, and the NFL was calling. Scouts and coaches took notice of his skills, and he began preparing for the next chapter in his life.

Despite the excitement of the NFL draft ahead, Justin cherished the memories he made during his college days at LSU. The friendships, the lessons learned, and the experiences he gained would stay with him forever. He knew that his time at LSU had shaped him not only as a football player but as a person.

College days at LSU were a transformative experience for Justin Jefferson. He worked hard, faced challenges, and celebrated victories, all while making lifelong memories with his teammates. As he prepared for the next step in his football journey, Justin carried with him the lessons learned and the joy of being part of a champion team. With his dreams in sight, he was ready to take on the world and show everyone what he could achieve. Justin Jefferson was on his way to becoming a star, and this was just the beginning of his incredible journey.

• CHAPTER 6: DRAFT DAY SURPRISE: THE EXCITING MOMENT JUSTIN JOINED THE NFL

Draft Day is one of the most thrilling and nerve-wracking events for college football players. For many athletes, it represents the culmination of years of hard work, dedication, and dreaming big. Justin Jefferson was no exception. After an outstanding college career at Louisiana State University (LSU), where he became one of the top wide receivers in the country, Justin was ready to take the next step in his football journey: entering the NFL.

The Build-Up to Draft Day

As Draft Day approached, Justin felt a mix of excitement and anxiety. He had spent countless hours preparing, training, and showcasing his skills in front of NFL scouts and coaches. He had participated in the NFL Combine, where he ran impressive drills and caught passes in front of top teams, all hoping to prove that he was ready for the professional level. His hard work was finally paying off, and now it was time to find out which team would select him.

Leading up to the draft, Justin received a lot of support from his family, friends, and coaches. They reminded him to stay calm and focused, regardless of where he was picked. Justin had a close-knit group that believed in him, and he felt grateful for their encouragement. He knew that whatever happened, he had already accomplished so much in his football journey.

The Big Day Arrives

Draft Day finally arrived, and Justin was buzzing with excitement. He chose to spend the day with his family at home, surrounded by the people who had always supported him. As he waited for the event to begin, he reflected on his journey—how far he had come from backyard games with his brothers to achieving his dreams at LSU.

When the draft started, Justin and his family gathered around the television, eagerly watching as the first few picks were announced. Teams were selecting players, and the tension in the room grew with each announcement. Justin's heart raced as he thought about the possibility of becoming a professional football player.

Waiting for the Call

As the first round progressed, Justin remained hopeful. Teams were picking their choices, and while some names were called, he was still waiting for his moment. Each time a wide receiver was selected, he felt a mix of emotions, excitement for his fellow players and a bit of anxiety about when his time would come. His family was supportive, cheering him on and reminding him to stay positive.

The first round continued, and Justin's anticipation turned into nervousness. He had worked so hard for this moment, and he wanted to be chosen by a team that believed in him. The clock ticked down for each pick, and with every passing moment, he hoped his name would be called soon.

The Moment of Truth

Finally, as the first round neared its end, Justin received a call from his agent. This was it—the moment he had been waiting for. The phone rang, and his heart pounded in his chest. His agent spoke quickly, filled with excitement, and Justin's eyes widened as he listened. The Minnesota Vikings were on the clock, and they were ready to select him!

When the Vikings officially called his name as their pick for the 22nd overall selection, the room erupted with joy. Justin's family hugged him tightly, tears of happiness in their eyes. It was a dream come true! Justin could hardly believe it—he was going to be a part of the Minnesota Vikings, a professional NFL team.

The Celebration

After the announcement, the excitement in the room was electric. Justin felt an overwhelming sense of joy and relief. His hard work had paid off, and all the sacrifices made along the way were worth it. They celebrated with laughter, cheers, and even a few happy tears. Justin was ready to embark on this new chapter in his life.

That night, the family gathered for a celebratory dinner. They reflected on Justin's journey, from playing football in the backyard to becoming an NFL player. Stories were shared, and everyone recounted the countless hours spent practicing and the support they had given each other throughout the years. Justin felt grateful for the love surrounding him and knew that this was just the beginning of something special.

Preparing for the NFL

In the days that followed, Justin was busy preparing for his new life as an NFL player. He attended introductory meetings with the Vikings and met his new teammates and coaches. The excitement was palpable, but so was the realization that he had a lot of work ahead of him. The NFL was a whole new level of competition, and Justin knew he had to be ready.

As he stepped into the Vikings' training facility for the first time, Justin was struck by the intensity and professionalism around him. He observed the training sessions and workouts, watching how the veterans approached their craft. It was a learning experience, and Justin was eager to soak up as much knowledge as he could.

Training Camp

Training camp was just around the corner, and Justin knew he had to put in his best effort to earn a spot on the team. He dedicated himself to training, focusing on improving his skills and building chemistry with his new quarterback. Practices were challenging, but Justin thrived in the competitive environment. He worked hard every day, determined to make an impact.

During camp, he began to showcase his talents. The coaches recognized his skills, and he quickly became a standout player among the rookies. Each practice brought new challenges, but Justin faced them head-on. He was determined to prove he could contribute to the team right away.

The First Game

As the season approached, Justin's excitement grew. He couldn't wait to step onto the field for his first NFL game. The anticipation was intense, and he spent time visualizing his performance. When the day finally arrived, he was ready to show everyone what he could do.

On game day, Justin felt a mix of nerves and exhilaration as he put on his Vikings uniform. He was filled with pride as he looked in the mirror, ready to represent his new team. As he ran onto the field with his teammates, the roar of the crowd filled his ears. It was a moment he would never forget.

In his debut game, Justin quickly made a name for himself. He caught several passes and made impactful plays, showcasing his speed and skill. The crowd erupted with cheers as he made his first touchdown catch, and he felt an overwhelming sense of accomplishment. All his hard work had led to this incredible moment.

As the season progressed, Justin continued to excel. He built a reputation as a reliable receiver, earning the respect of his teammates and coaches. The success he found in the NFL was a dream come true, and he was grateful for the support of his family and friends throughout his journey.

Draft Day was just the beginning for Justin Jefferson. The excitement of joining the NFL opened up a world of opportunities and challenges. As he stepped into this new chapter,

Justin was ready to embrace every moment. He had proven himself a dedicated athlete, and now it was time to shine on the professional stage. With his talent and determination, the sky was the limit for Justin Jefferson, and he was poised to make a significant impact in the world of football.

CHAPTER 7: THE GRIDDY DANCE: HOW JUSTIN'S CELEBRATION DANCE BECAME FAMOUS

When it comes to football, scoring a touchdown is one of the most exciting moments for players and fans alike. But what happens after a player scores? That's where the celebration comes in! Celebrations are a way for players to express their joy and excitement, and one player who has become famous for his celebrations is Justin Jefferson. His signature move, known as "The Griddy Dance," has captured the hearts of fans all over the world. Let's dive into how Justin created this fun and catchy dance and how it became a phenomenon!

The Spark of an Idea

Justin Jefferson grew up loving football. From a young age, he dreamed of playing in the NFL, and he worked hard to make that dream come true. He practiced his skills on the field, but he also had a fun side, he loved to dance! Justin would often show off his dance moves during practice, and it was clear that he had a natural talent for it. He wanted to combine his love for dancing with his love for football, and that's how The Griddy Dance started.

The idea for The Griddy Dance came from a popular dance move that was already making waves on social media. Justin noticed that many of his friends and fellow players were doing this dance, and he thought it would be a great way to celebrate after scoring a touchdown. He began to practice the move, adding his own flair to it. With every step, he made it more energetic and fun, ensuring it would be something everyone would enjoy.

The First Touchdown Celebration

Justin had his first chance to show off The Griddy Dance during a game while playing for the Minnesota Vikings. After scoring a touchdown, he couldn't contain his excitement. He immediately broke out into the dance, moving his arms and legs in a lively and catchy rhythm. The crowd erupted in cheers as they watched him celebrate his achievement. Justin's infectious energy brought smiles to everyone's faces, and the dance became an instant hit!

When Justin celebrated with The Griddy, fans loved it! People in the stands were clapping and cheering, and they even started to join in on the fun. The dance was easy to learn and full of energy, making it the perfect way to celebrate a touchdown. Justin's teammates were also excited about the dance, and soon they began to join in, creating a fun atmosphere on the field.

Social Media Sensation

As soon as Justin did The Griddy Dance on live television, people started sharing videos of it on social media. Platforms like TikTok, Instagram, and Twitter exploded with clips of his dance moves. Fans loved to recreate the dance, and it quickly became a trending challenge. Everyone, from kids to adults, wanted to try it out and show their version of The Griddy.

The Griddy Dance became more than just a celebration; it turned into a cultural phenomenon. Justin's creativity inspired countless fans to participate, and many celebrities even joined in the fun. Videos of people doing The Griddy flooded the internet, and Justin Jefferson became known not only as an amazing football player but also as a dance superstar.

Spreading the Joy

Justin loved seeing how much joy his dance brought to people. He enjoyed watching fans, friends, and even families come together to dance along. The Griddy Dance became a way for everyone to express themselves and have fun, especially during the exciting moments of a football game. Justin understood the importance of celebrating and having a good time, and he was thrilled that his dance could bring people together.

As more and more fans started to do The Griddy, Justin noticed that it wasn't just about scoring touchdowns anymore. The dance had become a symbol of happiness and celebration in football. Whether a player scored a touchdown or just made a fantastic play, doing The Griddy became a great way to celebrate the moment.

Justin's Impact on Football Culture

The Griddy Dance made a significant impact on football culture. Other players began to join in on the fun, and soon, it was common to see players celebrating with their own versions of The Griddy after making great plays. It wasn't just Justin; many players wanted to express their personalities and share their excitement with fans through dance. Justin had started a movement, and it brought even more excitement to the game.

Football fans started to look forward to celebrations as much as they looked forward to the touchdowns themselves. The Griddy Dance had a way of making games feel even more special, and fans loved to cheer for the players who celebrated in fun and creative ways. Justin had shown everyone that football could be both competitive and entertaining.

As The Griddy Dance became more popular, many kids wanted to learn it. Justin's influence inspired dance classes, social media challenges, and even school events where kids could show off their dance moves. Schools organized fun days where students could celebrate by dancing together, and The Griddy was always a favorite. Kids practiced the dance with their friends and challenged each other to see who could do it better.

Justin was thrilled to know that he had inspired so many young fans to embrace their creativity and have fun with dance. He often shared videos of kids doing The Griddy, and he loved to see how they made the dance their own. It brought him joy to see young fans light up with happiness while celebrating through dance.

As Justin continued to play in the NFL, The Griddy Dance remained a big part of his journey. He knew that celebrations were not just about showing off; they were about expressing joy, having fun, and sharing special moments with fans. The Griddy had become a celebration of the hard work and dedication that goes into playing football.

With every touchdown, Justin not only made fans cheer with excitement but also inspired them to express themselves and enjoy life. His journey from backyard games to the NFL showed everyone that dreams can come true, and sometimes, those dreams come with fun dances that spread happiness everywhere.

The Griddy Dance is more than just a celebration for Justin Jefferson; it's a symbol of joy and creativity in football. From its humble beginnings to becoming a global sensation, this dance has brought people together and made football games even more exciting. Justin's talent, hard work, and love for dance have created a legacy that will inspire future generations of young football players and dancers alike.

So, the next time you watch a football game and see a player celebrating with The Griddy, remember that it all started with a kid who loved to dance and had big dreams. Who knows? Maybe you'll create your own dance that will become famous one day too.

CHAPTER 8: LIFE AS A VIKINGS: JUSTIN JEFFERSON'S JOURNEY WITH THE MINNESOTA VIKINGS

When Justin Jefferson was drafted into the NFL, he joined one of the most exciting teams in football, the Minnesota Vikings! Being a part of the Vikings wasn't just about playing football; it was about being part of a family, facing challenges, and celebrating victories together. Let's dive into Justin's journey with the Vikings and what life is like as a player in the NFL!

The Big Move to Minnesota

After an impressive college career at Louisiana State University (LSU), Justin Jefferson was ready to take the next big step in his life. He was drafted by the Minnesota Vikings in the first round of the NFL Draft. This was a dream come true for Justin! He had worked hard, practiced every day, and now he was ready to play on the biggest stage of them all.

Moving to Minnesota was a big change for Justin. He left his home in Louisiana, which was warm and sunny, to live in a state known for its cold winters and beautiful lakes. But Justin was excited to experience new things and meet his new teammates. When he arrived in Minnesota, he was welcomed with open arms by fans and players alike, making him feel right at home.

Training Camp: The Beginning of the Journey

Before the season started, Justin participated in training camp with the Vikings. Training camp is where players come together to practice, learn plays, and prepare for the upcoming season. It was a time filled with hard work and determination, and Justin was ready to show everyone what he could do.

During training camp, Justin faced many challenges. He had to learn the playbook, which was filled with new plays and strategies. He also practiced running routes, catching passes, and working on his speed and agility. But Justin loved every minute of it! He pushed himself to improve every day, knowing that he wanted to be one of the best wide receivers in the league.

Making New Friends

One of the best parts of being a Viking was meeting new friends. Justin quickly became close with his teammates, including star players like Adam Thielen and Kirk Cousins. They practiced together, trained hard, and even shared laughs in the locker room. Justin learned that being part of a team meant supporting each other, both on and off the field.

The Vikings players often hung out outside of practice too. They would play video games, go to each other's houses, and bond over their shared love for football. This camaraderie helped them build trust and teamwork, which would be essential when they stepped onto the field during games.

Game Day Excitement

As the season began, game days became some of the most exciting times for Justin. The atmosphere at U.S. Bank Stadium, the Vikings' home, was electric! Fans filled the stands, wearing purple and gold, cheering for their team with all their hearts. The energy in the stadium was contagious, and Justin loved being in the spotlight.

Before each game, Justin would go through a special routine. He listened to music to pump himself up, put on his uniform, and took a moment to focus. Once he stepped onto the field, he could feel the excitement in the air. Every game was an opportunity to showcase his skills and help his team win.

Scoring Touchdowns and Celebrating

During his first season, Justin quickly made a name for himself. He worked hard in practice, and when it was game time, he gave it his all. He caught passes, made amazing plays, and scored touchdowns, much to the delight of Vikings fans. Each time he crossed the end zone, he celebrated with his signature Griddy dance, which made fans cheer even louder!

Celebrating touchdowns was one of Justin's favorite moments. It was a time to share joy with his teammates and the fans. After scoring, Justin would often run over to the sidelines to high-five his coaches and celebrate with his teammates. They would all gather to do a fun dance together, creating a bond that brought them closer.

Facing Challenges

Life as a Viking wasn't always easy. Justin faced challenges along the way, from tough losses to injuries. There were moments when he felt frustrated and disappointed, but he learned that being part of a team meant sticking together during tough times. His teammates supported him, encouraging him to keep pushing forward.

Justin also learned the importance of perseverance. Every setback was an opportunity to learn and grow. Whether it was working harder in practice or focusing on recovery after an injury, Justin understood that challenges made him stronger. He used these experiences to become a better player and a better teammate.

Giving Back to the Community

Being a Viking wasn't just about playing football; it was also about giving back to the community. Justin and his teammates took part in various events and programs to help those in need. They visited schools, organized charity events, and participated in community service projects. Justin loved being a role model for kids and inspiring them to follow their dreams.

During these events, Justin would share his story and encourage kids to work hard in school and sports. He wanted them to know that with dedication and perseverance, they could achieve their dreams, just like he did. This connection with the community made Justin feel even more proud to be a Viking.

Learning from Coaches

Another important part of Justin's life as a Viking was learning from his coaches. They were there to guide him and help him improve every step of the way. The coaching staff taught him valuable lessons about strategy, teamwork, and discipline. Justin listened closely to their advice and applied it during games and practices.

One of his coaches even helped him refine his catching techniques, making sure he could snag those tricky passes. The feedback and support from his coaches played a significant role in Justin's development as a player and helped him become a key part of the Vikings' success.

Celebrating Successes Together

As the season progressed, Justin and the Vikings celebrated many successes. They worked hard, played well together, and enjoyed some thrilling victories. Every win felt special, and Justin knew that it was all about teamwork and dedication. He cherished these moments, as they created memories that would last a lifetime.

After a big win, the Vikings would celebrate as a team. They would gather in the locker room, play music, and enjoy the victory together. Justin loved these moments, knowing that all the hard work paid off. It wasn't just about the wins; it was about the bond they formed as a team.

As Justin Jefferson continued his journey with the Minnesota Vikings, he knew that the future was bright. He had already achieved so much, but he was determined to keep working hard and striving for greatness. With each practice and game, he aimed to improve his skills and be the best player he could be.

Justin also hoped to inspire young fans everywhere. He wanted them to know that dreams come true with dedication and hard work. Whether playing football, dancing, or pursuing any passion, he encouraged kids to believe in themselves and never give up.

Life as a Viking was filled with excitement, challenges, and memorable moments for Justin Jefferson. From training camp to game days, he experienced the joy of being part of a team and the thrill of scoring touchdowns. Along the way, he learned valuable lessons about teamwork, perseverance, and giving back to the community.

As Justin continued to shine on the field, he inspired young fans to dream big and work hard. His journey showed everyone that with passion and dedication, anything is possible. So, whether you're a football player, dancer, or simply chasing your dreams, remember that you can achieve greatness just like Justin Jefferson.

● CHAPTER 9: TOUCHDOWNS AND RECORDS: JUSTIN'S AMAZING FOOTBALL MOMENTS AND BREAKING RECORDS

Justin Jefferson is not just any football player; he is a superstar wide receiver known for his incredible talent and amazing plays on the field. From the moment he started playing, Justin has created countless unforgettable moments, scoring touchdowns and breaking records along the way. Let's take a look at some of his most exciting achievements and what makes him such a remarkable player!

Early Touchdowns: Making a Name for Himself

When Justin first joined the Minnesota Vikings, he was determined to make an impact. He was ready to show everyone what he could do! In his very first game, Justin caught his first touchdown pass in front of cheering fans at U.S.

Bank Stadium. It was a thrilling moment for him, and he felt an adrenaline rush as he crossed the end zone. He couldn't believe he had scored in his first NFL game!

As the season went on, Justin continued to impress everyone with his skills. He made amazing catches, dodged defenders, and showcased his speed. Every time he scored a touchdown, it brought joy to his teammates and Vikings fans. Justin's ability to find the end zone quickly made him a fan favorite!

Breaking Records in His Rookie Year

Justin's rookie year was nothing short of incredible. He was breaking records left and right! One of his biggest achievements was setting a new record for the most receiving yards by a rookie in a single season. This record had stood for years, but Justin was determined to surpass it. With each game, he got closer to this milestone, and every time he caught a pass, he was one step closer to making history.

In a thrilling game against the New Orleans Saints, Justin broke the record for the most receiving yards in a game by a Vikings player, showcasing his talent and determination. His teammates cheered him on, and the crowd erupted with excitement. Justin felt proud to achieve such a significant milestone and knew he was on his way to becoming a football star.

The Importance of Teamwork

While Justin is a fantastic player, he knows that football is a team sport. Every touchdown he scored was a result of teamwork and support from his fellow Vikings. His quarterback, Kirk Cousins, trusted him to make big plays, and their connection on the field was electric. Justin often talks about how important it is to work together with his teammates, whether it's in practice or during games.

During practices, they worked hard to improve their skills and develop plays. They practiced different routes and strategies to outsmart the opposing teams. Justin knew that by working together, they could achieve great things. The Vikings were not just a team; they were a family who supported each other through thick and thin.

Celebrating Touchdowns with Style

Every time Justin scored a touchdown, he had a special way of celebrating that made fans smile. He created a unique celebration called the "Griddy Dance." After crossing the goal line, Justin would do this fun and catchy dance that quickly became a sensation. Fans loved it so much that they started to copy his moves!

The Griddy Dance became a way for Justin to express his joy after scoring and connect with the fans. It brought a sense of excitement to the game, and everyone would cheer even louder when they saw him dance. Justin's fun spirit and enthusiasm made watching him play even more enjoyable for kids and adults alike.

More Records and Achievements

As the seasons progressed, Justin continued to break records and achieve new milestones. He became one of the top wide receivers in the NFL, earning awards and recognition for his outstanding performance. Justin was selected to the Pro Bowl, which is an exciting event where the best players in the league come together to showcase their skills. It was a dream come true for him!

In addition to personal achievements, Justin contributed to the Vikings' success as a team. He played a vital role in helping the Vikings reach the playoffs, and every game brought new opportunities for him to shine. Justin's hard work, dedication, and passion for the game inspired not only his teammates but also young fans who looked up to him.

Beyond the records and touchdowns, what makes Justin truly special is his ability to inspire others. He has a positive attitude and never gives up, no matter the challenges he faces. When things don't go as planned during a game, Justin encourages his teammates to keep pushing forward. He understands that everyone has tough days, but the key is to stay focused and work together as a team.

Justin often shares his journey with young fans, telling them that dreams can come true with hard work and determination. He wants kids to believe in themselves and pursue their passions, whether it's in sports or other activities. His story is a reminder that with effort and teamwork, amazing things can happen!

Justin knows that being a role model comes with responsibilities. He uses his platform to give back to the community and help those in need. Whether it's visiting schools, participating in charity events, or supporting youth programs, Justin loves making a difference in the lives of others.

Through his charitable work, Justin inspires kids to be kind, work hard, and strive for their dreams. He understands that he can use his success to help others, and he takes this responsibility seriously. By giving back, he shows that football is not just about winning games; it's also about making a positive impact on the world.

As Justin Jefferson continues his journey in the NFL, he has many goals in mind. He wants to keep breaking records, scoring touchdowns, and becoming an even better player. He aims to lead his team to victory and inspire young athletes everywhere to follow their dreams.

With each passing season, Justin knows that challenges may arise, but he is ready to face them head-on. He believes in hard work, perseverance, and the power of teamwork. Justin's dedication to the game and his love for football will drive him to achieve even greater things in the future.

Justin Jefferson's journey in the NFL has been filled with amazing moments, touchdowns, and records that will be remembered for years to come. His story is not just about his achievements on the field; it's also about the friendships he has built, the challenges he has faced, and the inspiration he provides to kids everywhere.

As young fans look up to Justin, they see that with hard work and a positive attitude, anything is possible. Whether it's scoring a touchdown, dancing in the end zone, or breaking records, Justin Jefferson is a shining example of what it means to be a true champion on and off the field.

• CHAPTER 10: DREAMS KEEP GROWING

Every great journey begins with a dream, and for Justin Jefferson, dreams have always played a huge part in his life. As a young boy, Justin had big dreams of becoming a football star. He didn't just want to play for fun; he wanted to make it to the NFL and become one of the best wide receivers in the game. This is the story of how Justin's dreams grew and flourished, leading him to become the superstar he is today.

A Young Boy with Big Dreams

From a young age, Justin was surrounded by sports. He grew up in a family that loved football, and his dad was a football coach. Watching his father coach inspired Justin to play. He would often watch games on television, imagining himself making incredible catches and scoring touchdowns. As he saw his favorite players on the screen, Justin felt excitement bubbling inside him. He wanted to be just like them!

Justin would spend hours outside, tossing a football around with his brothers. They would create their own games, pretending to be their favorite athletes. They used their imagination to turn their backyard into a football field, where anything was possible. The more he played, the more his dreams grew. Each catch and every touchdown felt like a step closer to making his dream come true.

Finding Inspiration

Justin didn't just look up to his family; he also found inspiration from other athletes. Players like Randy Moss and Odell Beckham Jr. became his role models. He admired their skills, their moves, and the way they celebrated after scoring. He dreamed of one day being just as good as them. Whenever he watched their highlights, he felt motivated to practice harder and improve his game.

As he practiced, Justin learned the importance of dedication. He knew that dreaming big was just the beginning; he needed to work hard to turn those dreams into reality. He practiced every day, honing his skills and pushing himself to become a better player. Each practice was a chance to learn and grow.

Overcoming Challenges

Like all dreamers, Justin faced challenges along the way. There were days when he struggled and felt like giving up. Sometimes he didn't play as well as he wanted, or he faced tough opponents who seemed bigger and stronger. However, Justin remembered his dreams and the reasons he started playing football. He realized that challenges were just a part of the journey. Instead of letting them stop him, he used them to fuel his determination.

Justin learned that it's okay to make mistakes. What matters is how you respond to them.

Instead of being discouraged, he practiced even harder. With every setback, he grew stronger and more determined. He would often tell himself that dreams are like seeds: they need time, care, and effort to grow.

The Importance of Support

Throughout his journey, Justin was lucky to have a strong support system. His family cheered him on at every game, celebrating his victories and comforting him in defeat. His friends also encouraged him, joining him in practices and games. They reminded him that he wasn't alone in his dreams.

His coaches played a crucial role too. They taught him valuable lessons about teamwork, perseverance, and sportsmanship. They believed in his talent and pushed him to reach his full potential. With their guidance, Justin became not only a better player but also a better teammate. He learned that dreams are more enjoyable when shared with others who believe in you.

Making It to High School

As Justin entered high school, his dreams continued to grow. He joined the football team and worked hard to make a name for himself. It was a new challenge, but Justin was ready. He practiced day and night, focusing on his skills and building relationships with his teammates.

In high school, he had the chance to showcase his talent on a bigger stage. He quickly became one of the top players on his team, catching the attention of coaches and scouts. Every game was an opportunity to shine and show what he could do. Justin loved the thrill of competition and the excitement of making big plays. He knew he was getting closer to his dreams.

The Road to College

As Justin's high school career progressed, college recruiters began to notice him. They saw his potential and talent, and Justin felt the excitement of his dreams coming to life. Receiving offers from different colleges made him feel proud and hopeful for the future.

Ultimately, Justin chose to play for Louisiana State University (LSU), a place known for its amazing football program. This was a big step for him, and he was determined to make the most of it. He continued to work hard, pushing himself to learn and improve. The competition was fierce, but Justin thrived under pressure. He was determined to make his mark and show everyone that he belonged there.

Achieving His Dreams

At LSU, Justin blossomed as a player. He played alongside other talented athletes and learned from experienced coaches. He broke records and made incredible plays that thrilled fans. With every game, his dreams felt more tangible. He was living the life he had always imagined!

His hard work paid off when he became a star at LSU, and he earned a spot in the NFL Draft. This was the moment he had been waiting for. The excitement of being selected by the Minnesota Vikings filled him with joy. He realized that his dreams were finally coming true. He was on his way to becoming a professional football player!

Continuing to Dream Big

Even after reaching the NFL, Justin knew that dreams don't stop growing. He set new goals for himself and continued to work hard every day. He wanted to be the best wide receiver in the league and help his team win championships. Justin also understood that he had a responsibility to inspire others. He wanted young fans to know that dreams can come true if you believe in yourself and work hard.

Justin often shares his story with kids, encouraging them to pursue their dreams no matter how big or small. He believes that every child has the potential to achieve greatness. By sharing his journey, he hopes to motivate others to keep dreaming and to never give up.

Justin Jefferson's journey is a testament to the power of dreams. From a young boy playing in the backyard to an NFL star, Justin's story shows that with hard work, determination, and support, dreams can grow and flourish. His life reminds us that it's important to keep believing in ourselves and to chase our dreams with all our hearts. Just like Justin, every child has the potential to achieve their dreams and make them a reality.

• CONCLUSION

Justin Jefferson's journey from a kid with big dreams to an NFL superstar is truly inspiring. His story teaches us that with hard work, determination, and the support of loved ones, anything is possible. Justin didn't just wake up one day and become a football star. It took years of dedication, practice, and overcoming challenges to reach the heights of his career. His success didn't come easy, but he showed us that when you believe in yourself and keep pushing forward, amazing things can happen.

A Kid with Big Dreams

From the very beginning, Justin's story was about more than just football. It was about a young boy who dared to dream big. Justin wasn't afraid to set high goals for himself, even when those around him didn't know if he could make it. His love for the game and his desire to become the best fueled his drive. Whether it was playing in the backyard with his brothers or practicing with his high school team, Justin always gave his all.

His dreams didn't stop growing, either. Every new challenge became an opportunity to learn and improve. With every practice session, game, and season, Justin moved closer to his goal of becoming a professional football player. He never let obstacles stand in his way, and his dedication paid off.

One of the most important lessons from Justin's story is the value of hard work. Throughout his journey, Justin faced tough opponents, injuries, and times when things didn't go as planned. But instead of giving up, he kept working. He practiced every day, making sure he improved in every area of his game. He listened to his coaches, learned from his mistakes, and always pushed himself to be better.

Hard work is something anyone can apply to their own lives, no matter what their dreams are.

Justin's story shows that while talent is important, it's the effort you put in that truly makes the difference. Whether you want to be a football player, an artist, a scientist, or anything else, working hard and staying focused is what will help you achieve your dreams.

Justin's journey wasn't without its challenges. From not being heavily recruited out of high school to working hard to prove himself at LSU, he faced setbacks along the way. But instead of seeing these as reasons to give up, Justin saw them as opportunities to grow. He learned to handle criticism, push through difficult moments, and come out stronger on the other side.

This is a valuable lesson for all of us. Life will always have challenges, but how we respond to them is what matters most. Justin didn't let disappointment or failure stop him. He stayed determined, focused, and kept moving forward. This resilience helped him reach his goals and become the player he is today.

Justin's dream of playing in the NFL came true when he was drafted by the Minnesota Vikings. This was the moment he had worked toward his entire life. But even then, his story didn't stop. Justin continued to set new goals and push himself to achieve even more. His incredible skills, dedication, and positive attitude helped him make an impact on the field almost immediately. In his rookie season, he broke records and became one of the best wide receivers in the league.

His famous Griddy dance became a celebration not just for him, but for football fans everywhere. It was a fun way for Justin to express his excitement, and it quickly became a signature move. Fans loved it, and soon, people all over the world were trying to do the Griddy!

One of the most important parts of Justin's story is how he inspires others. Justin didn't just achieve his own dreams; he also became a role model for kids who want to follow in his footsteps. He shows young people that no matter where you come from or what challenges you face, you can achieve great things if you believe in yourself and work hard.

Justin's story encourages kids to chase their dreams, be kind, and never give up. Whether you want to play football or do something completely different, his journey reminds us that with the right mindset and effort, anything is possible.

Even though Justin has achieved so much already, he continues to dream big. His journey is far from over. Every season, he looks for new ways to improve, new records to break, and new ways to help his team succeed. Justin's dedication to football and his love for the game are clear in everything he does. He is always striving to be better and to inspire others along the way.

For Justin, the sky's the limit. His story is a reminder that dreams don't stop once you've achieved them. They keep growing, just like Justin. He continues to set new goals and push himself to reach even greater heights. His journey is one of perseverance, passion, and joy, and it's far from finished.

Justin Jefferson's story teaches us that dreams are powerful. They are the seeds that can grow into something incredible if you nurture them with hard work and belief. Justin's journey from a kid playing in his backyard to an NFL superstar is proof that no dream is too big. He shows us that with dedication, resilience, and a positive attitude, we can achieve anything we set our minds to.

For kids reading his story, Justin's life is a shining example of what it means to dream big, work hard, and never give up. Whether your dream is to be a football star like Justin or to do something else entirely, his journey inspires us all to keep going, no matter the challenges we face.

Justin Jefferson's rise to football fame is more than just a sports story; it's a story about following your heart, working hard, and believing in yourself. Justin's determination, passion, and ability to overcome challenges have made him a role model for kids everywhere. He has shown that with big dreams and even bigger effort, you can achieve great things.

As Justin continues his football career, one thing is certain: his dreams will keep growing, and so will his impact on the game and the people who look up to him. His story reminds us that no matter how big or small your dreams are, they are worth chasing. Just like Justin Jefferson, you too can dance your way to greatness.

Made in the USA
Monee, IL
29 October 2024

68967370R00059